Hayley Wickenheiser
Born to Play

Elizabeth Etue

Kids Can Press

To my precious great-niece Olivia — may she come to love
women's hockey as much as I do.

Acknowledgments

I want to thank Hayley Wickenheiser for her generosity. Her diligence in acquiring
photos, especially from her family and friends, is greatly appreciated. Thank you to Allie,
Sam, Susan and Tony Biglieri and the Leaside Wildcats Atom BB for their feedback
and keen interest in the book. Special thanks to my editor Liz MacLeod, publisher
Valerie Hussey and all the enthusiastic women's hockey fans at Kids Can Press.

And bravo to all those courageous girls and their parents who love the game
and continue to play despite the many obstacles.

Kids Can Press acknowledges the financial support of
the Government of Ontario, through the Ontario Media
Development Corporation's Ontario Book Initiative; the
Ontario Arts Council; the Canada Council for the Arts;
and the Government of Canada, through the BPIDP, for
our publishing activity.

Published in Canada by Kids Can Press Ltd. 29 Birch Avenue Toronto, ON M4V 1E2	Published in the U.S. by Kids Can Press Ltd. 2250 Military Road Tonawanda, NY 14150

www.kidscanpress.com

Edited by Elizabeth MacLeod
Designed by Julia Naimska
Cover photograph: Hockey Canada/Gerry Thomas
Printed and bound in China

This book is limp sewn with a drawn-on cover.

CM PA 05 0 9 8 7 6 5 4 3 2 1

Library and Archives Canada Cataloguing in Publication

Etue, Elizabeth Anne Agnes, [date]
    Hayley Wickenheiser : born to play / written by Elizabeth
Etue.

ISBN 1-55337-791-5

1. Hockey players — Canada — Biography. I. Title.

GV848.5.W52E88 2005   796.962'092
C2004-906028-7

Photo credits

Every reasonable effort has been made to trace ownership of,
and give accurate credit to, copyrighted material. Information
that would enable the publisher to correct any discrepancies
in future editions would be appreciated.

Abbreviations
t = top; b = bottom; c = center; l = left; r = right

p. 3: (t) Marilyn Wickenheiser Collection, (b) Jussi Salo;
p. 4: Hockey Canada/Dave Sandford; **p. 5:** (t) Jussi Salo, (b)
Hockey Canada/Dave Sandford; **p. 6:** (l, r) Hayley Wickenheiser
Collection; **p. 7:** (t) Hayley Wickenheiser Collection, (b) Marilyn
Wickenheiser Collection; **p. 8:** Marilyn Wickenheiser Collection;
p. 9: (t, c, b) Marilyn Wickenheiser Collection; **p. 10:** (l, r)
Marilyn Wickenheiser Collection; **p. 11:** (t, b) Marilyn
Wickenheiser Collection; **p. 12:** (t) Hayley Wickenheiser
Collection, (b) Hockey Canada/Gerry Thomas; **p. 13:** (t, c, b)
Hayley Wickenheiser Collection; **p. 14:** (t) Marilyn Wickenheiser
Collection, (b) Hayley Wickenheiser Collection; **p. 15:** (t) Hayley
Wickenheiser Collection, (b) Marilyn Wickenheiser Collection;
p. 16: (t) Hayley Wickenheiser Collection, (b) Hockey Canada/
Gerry Thomas; **p. 17:** Gerry Thomas; **p. 18:** (t) CP Photo
Archive/Mike Ridewood, (b) CP Photo Archive/Paul Chiasson;
p. 19: (l) Marilyn Wickenheiser Collection, (r) CP Photo Archive;
p. 20: Len Redkoles; **p. 21:** (l, r) Hayley Wickenheiser Collection;
p. 22: (t, b) Hayley Wickenheiser Collection; **p. 23:** (l) Marilyn
Wickenheiser Collection, (r) Rick Moore; **p. 24:** (l) Marilyn
Wickenheiser Collection, (r) Hockey Canada/Gerry Thomas;
p. 25: (t, b) Hayley Wickenheiser Collection; **p. 26:** (t, b)
Gerry Thomas; **p. 27:** (t, b) Gerry Thomas; **p. 28:** (t) Marilyn
Wickenheiser Collection, (b) Hayley Wickenheiser Collection;
p. 29: Gerry Thomas; **p. 30:** (t) Hockey Canada/Jeff Vinnick, (b)
Jussi Salo; **p. 31:** (t) Gerry Thomas, (b) Hayley Wickenheiser
Collection; **p. 32:** Jukka Rautio; **p. 33:** (t, b) Jukka Rautio;
p. 34: (t) Jussi Salo, (c) Camilla Nilson, (b) Jukka Rautio; **p. 35:**
Jukka Rautio; **p. 36:** Mark Cresswell/Think Digital; **p. 37:** (t, b)
Hockey Canada/Dave Sandford; **p. 38:** Rick Madonik/The Toronto
Star; **p. 39:** (t) Mike Ridewood, (c) Karen McFadyen, (b) Hayley
Wickenheiser Collection; **p. 40:** Dale MacMillan.

Kids Can Press is a *corus*™ Entertainment company

Contents

Superstar

Meet Hayley Wickenheiser, a superstar hockey player. She surprised everyone when she became the youngest player ever to make Canada's national women's team — she was just 15 years old.

Hayley played on Canada's first Olympic women's hockey team at the 1998 games in Nagano. In 2002 she was the top goal scorer at the Olympic Games in Salt Lake City and led the team to its first Olympic gold medal. And she was the second Canadian woman ever to compete in both the summer and winter Olympics. Hayley played for Canada's national softball team at the Sydney Games in 2000.

Hayley battles with the Team USA goaltender in the final game at the 2002 Olympics.

But Hayley is much more than simply a talented athlete. She is an extraordinary combination of skills, intelligence and fierce determination who is always testing herself. She continually pushes to be better.

Winning an Olympic gold medal wasn't enough for Hayley. In Finland during 2003, she became the first North American woman to play forward for a men's pro team. Her desire to excel propelled her to new heights as a female hockey player.

After a game in the Finnish men's pro league in 2003, Hayley had to deal with lots of questions from the media.

Hayley Wickenheiser is living the dream of many elite athletes. She plays hockey at the highest level possible. She is also young, gifted and willing to make huge sacrifices to be the best. Her story is about courage, bold action and ambitious dreams.

Winning the gold medal at the 2002 Olympic Games was one of Hayley's proudest moments.

First Skates

For Hayley, the hockey rink was the heart of her hometown, Shaunavon, Saskatchewan. "I loved to be at the rink," Hayley says. "Life was at the arena."

Hayley was born on August 12, 1978. She watched her first hockey game in 1980 when she was two years old. When she was three, Hayley's dad built a rink behind their house. She played shinny hockey there with the neighborhood kids and her younger brother, Ross, and sister, Jane.

Hayley spent hours watching her hockey heroes Wayne Gretzky and Mark Messier on television. She would later practice their moves on her backyard rink. Lots of other sports kept Hayley busy, too, including softball, volleyball, track and soccer. She even tried figure skating for a few years.

But the sport Hayley wanted to play most was hockey. The lack of girls' teams in Shaunavon made things difficult for five-year-old Hayley. That problem was solved when she and a couple of other girls made the boys' team coached by her dad.

"My dad was my first mentor. He taught me all about hockey when I was growing up."

Five-year-old Hayley in costume for her first Ice Carnival in Shaunavon, Saskatchewan.

Hayley loved being on the ice, sometimes spending three or four hours at the rink playing hockey and practicing figure skating.

With all that extra skating and practicing, Hayley soon became the top scorer on her team. Like most kids, she only wanted to score goals. Sometimes she forgot about the importance of defence. So her father put her on defence to teach her to "read" the game and understand each player's role. She played that position for five years — and still won league-scoring titles. At ten, Hayley moved up to the Shaunavon Badgers team.

Hockey meant the world to Hayley. "I felt nothing was going to stop me from playing hockey," she remembers. "I practiced signing autographs at home. I was going to play in the NHL."

Class photo day at Shaunavon Public School for second-grader Hayley.

Hayley (right) and her brother, Ross, stickhandling on their backyard rink in 1988.

Ambitious Dreams

Since Hayley was scoring lots of goals, her coach moved her to forward. With her speed, shooting skills and intense passion for the game, she won the Most Valuable Player award for several years. Hayley also became a target for opposing players, who slashed and hit her. No one wanted a girl to be the best player in a boys' league.

Hayley knew there were advantages to playing with boys. They were usually more skilled at hockey than girls since they started playing at a younger age. It wasn't easy being the only girl and one of the best players, but Hayley realized that competing with boys forced her to play better and smarter.

Being the only girl meant Hayley always had to change in a separate room from her teammates. But she never complained. "From a very young age, I learned to develop a thick skin and not listen to the critical opinion of others," she says.

Hayley (back row, center) was the only girl on the Shaunavon Tom Thumbs. Her brother, Ross (front row, far left), also played on the team, and her father (back right) was head coach.

Best friends Hayley and Danielle Mitchell joking around at home.

In 1990 hockey changed dramatically for Hayley when her family moved to Calgary. A new female coach, Shannon Miller, had just started the first girls' team there. The skills Hayley had developed during her years of playing with boys quickly secured her a spot on Coach Miller's team.

Finally Hayley had a chance to really be a part of a team — she could even change in the same dressing room. Coach Miller has a

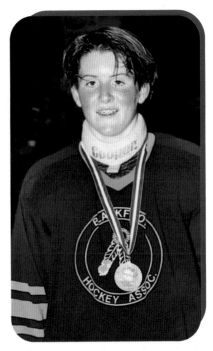

Hayley's first girls' team, the Blackfoot Cougar Bantams, won gold at the Western Shield tournament in 1991.

vivid memory of eleven-year-old Hayley. "She was a very spirited kid, a lot of energy about her," Miller recalls. "She just couldn't wait to get out on the ice."

The year 1991 marked another huge event for Hayley: playing in the Canada Winter Games. She was the only 12 year old chosen for Alberta's women's hockey team — the other players were all 16 to 18 years old. Would Hayley be able to keep up?

The nine-year-old high-scoring defender for the Shaunavon Tom Thumbs.

While training for Team Alberta, Hayley began to understand what it meant to be an elite athlete and to receive advice on subjects such as weight training, nutrition and mental attitude.

"I noticed a huge improvement in my power and speed," says Hayley. "I just wanted to skate faster than a jet plane, but I learned I had to take care of my body and manage things like fatigue and recovery."

Team Alberta was made up of players who were bigger than Hayley. She stood less than 1.5 m (5 ft.) tall and weighed 54 kg (120 lb.). But Hayley not only kept up with her teammates, she scored three goals, including blasting a slapshot to score the winning goal in the gold-medal game. That won her the Most Valuable Player award.

After Team Alberta won the 1991 Canada Winter Games, Hayley and her mom smile for the camera.

Hayley's success at the Canada Winter Games marked a turning point for her. She was thrilled to be invited to a national team selection camp the following year. This camp was a chance to skate with her heroes!

Twelve-year-old Hayley, ready to win with her Calgary girls' team playing in the boys' bantam league.

The Northwest Bruins AA Bantam boys' team had one girl on the roster — Hayley (front row, second from the left).

To keep her skills sharp, in 1993 Hayley played on a boys' Bantam AA team, the Calgary Northwest Bruins. Now she coped with body checking and much faster players. "These guys were bigger and stronger, so they forced me to play smarter," Hayley says. "I was the only girl out there so I had something to prove."

Hayley had exceptional hockey skills for her age and an intense desire to succeed, but she still needed to learn the mental part of the game. "I was overanxious," she admits. "I wasn't good away from the puck. I got too emotional, too excited and went too fast."

Most Valuable Player plus Most Dedicated Player in the boys' Bantam AA league in Calgary and the only girl in the league: Hayley Wickenheiser.

Team Canada

At the 1993 national team selection camp, Hayley was nervous. "I was on the ice with Canada's best players. They were my heroes," she remembers. "My hands were sweaty and my stomach was in knots during the first practice."

But she wowed the coaches. "Hayley plays like a 25 year old," Coach Les Lawton said. "She's got a lot of polish, a lot of natural ability and intensity that you don't find in [older] players. In fact, she was a step ahead of many players here."

Heading to a practice for the 1994 World Championship with Assistant Coach Shannon Miller.

Watching the play at the 1997 World Championship.

Thirty-nine players were trying out for Team Canada, all of them older and more experienced than Hayley. The odds were against someone so young making the team. She had just turned 15 when she became the youngest player ever to claim a spot on Canada's national team!

Her teammates started calling her "Highchair Hayley" because she was the baby of the squad.

"They treated me like a little sister," remembers Hayley, grinning. Margot Page, a high school math teacher, turned out to be a perfect roommate, especially when Hayley needed help with her homework. Teammates Stacy Wilson, France St. Louis and Margot Page were Hayley's role models. "It was such a team concept. We were all on a mission," she says. "A lot was expected of us."

Team Canada warms up with aerobics at the 1994 World Championship.

This was the first time Hayley had received such high-quality coaching. "There was a lot more preparation, a lot higher standard expected from players. When things weren't going well, I was usually trying too hard — trying to do too much, not trusting my teammates."

Hayley's impact on the team increased with each competition. In 1995 she was named to the all-star team at the Pacific Rim Tournament. At the 1997 Women's World Hockey Championship, Hayley was Canada's top scorer and made the all-star team.

At the 1996 Pacific Rim Tournament, Hayley gets ready for a pass in the final game against the United States.

Off the Ice

It was tough for Hayley to squeeze in home and school activities while playing hockey for both the national team and a local team. There was no hockey if chores weren't done — that was the rule at the Wickenheiser household.

Hayley's bedroom was covered with posters of her heroes, such as NHL player Mark Messier and Olympic track star Diane Jones Konihowski. She read biographies about successful people, including Nelson Mandela and Wayne Gretzky, and posted quotes all over her bedroom. "I was interested in people who were exceptional," Hayley remembers. "I learned that they have incredible discipline and commitment, huge passion for what they do and one single focus."

Hayley (wearing cap) clowning around after a fastball tournament in 1989.

Besides chores, school and hockey, Hayley made time for music. She studied piano until she was 13 and learned to play many songs by heart. In 1997 Hayley and three national team members started a band called "Funsion." "It didn't last long because no one had time to practice," she laughs.

Three of the Bishop Carroll High School basketball players in 1994.

14

Hayley loved most sports. She played volleyball, basketball and fastball in high school along with hockey. "I didn't go to parties much. I wasn't hanging out at the mall. For me it was hockey, training and school. It wasn't a sacrifice, it was the time of my life."

Hayley worked on a self-directed study program, finishing high school in two and a half years instead of three. Her goal was medical school. "I have always been fascinated with medicine," says Hayley. "I like the idea of helping people and also working on the human

Rock climbing with friends Sandy Foster (left) and Judy Diduck (right) at Kananaskis, Alberta, in 1997.

body. Things happen fast in medicine and you encounter a lot of pressure situations like in hockey, which appeals to me."

But university would have to wait. In 1998, the national women's team was going to be the first Canadian women's hockey team to play in the Olympics. Hayley was determined to be there.

Christmas 1995 with the Wickenheisers: Hayley; sister, Jane; Mom; brother, Ross; and Dad.

Making History

In August 1997, 19-year-old Hayley began training for the Nagano Olympics. This was full-time hockey!

Hayley was one of 40 players working to make the Olympic team. A typical training day meant getting up at 7:00 AM for breakfast and a few hours of practice, then lunch and a nap. After that, it was back to the gym for weight training, bike riding or yoga.

The team trained six days a week, but the coach wasn't happy with their play. "The training felt like

Team Canada playing shinny hockey at Emerald Lake, British Columbia, before heading to the 1998 Olympics.

military camp," Hayley says. "We weren't performing so Coach Miller made us do lots of extra work."

On February 10, 1998, the team arrived in Nagano, Japan. For Hayley it was thrilling to be one of the first female hockey players at the Olympics. "We were the first group of women who had a chance to have this historic impact on the game. My biggest job was to play to the best of my abilities."

The media and fans were clamoring to talk to 19-year-old Hayley, the youngest player and rising star on the team. It made Hayley feel as if the whole world was watching.

Team Canada had less than four days to practice and recover from the stress of travel. However, the team won its first three games against Japan, Sweden and Finland. During the game against Sweden, Hayley broke a bone in her right elbow and strained ligaments in her left knee as a result of a collision.

Hayley had to skate with intense pain but wanted to keep playing. "I had my elbow frozen before the games, so it was hard to shoot the puck with any power," Hayley sighs.

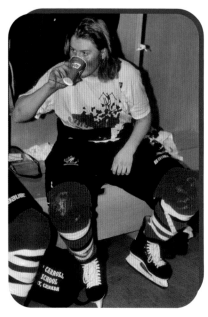

Hayley recovers after a hectic practice with Team Canada in 1997.

Despite being grabbed by a Japanese player, Hayley stays focused.

In the next game, the team lost 7–4 against the United States. Hayley was frustrated despite scoring two goals. "It was a crucial game," Hayley says. "We made some mistakes and let the momentum slip away. I remember being mad because of the way we lost." The team rebounded in the semi-final game, beating Finland 4–2. That win earned them a place in the gold-medal game against the United States.

Checking an American player in the final game at the Nagano Olympics.

With teammates Stacy Wilson (left) and Manon Rhéaume (center) after arriving at the Athletes' Village in 1998.

"I remember game day didn't feel like a good day," recalls Hayley, shaking her head. "There was incredible pressure and anxiety. I felt that if I didn't play my best game, the team wouldn't win. I know now you have to trust the team."

Hayley still remembers the game's last minutes when the score was 2–1 for the States: "I was on the ice for the last five seconds of the game. It was like slow motion seeing the puck go into our empty net. Losing had never entered my mind. I was in total shock."

So was the rest of Team Canada. Players were crying, but Hayley didn't want to show her feelings. "On the ice I told myself I would not shed a tear in front of the world or the

A disappointed Hayley with her parents after the Nagano Olympics.

U.S." She sat in the dressing room for the next two hours and cried. "I felt totally numb — like I'd let everyone in Canada down. I think we all promised ourselves we would never make the same mistake again."

Goal! Team Canada celebrates during the semi-final at the 1998 Olympics.

Only the Best

After Nagano, Hayley returned to Canada disappointed with her Olympic experience and ready for something different. She decided to follow up on a conversation she'd had in Nagano with Bobby Clarke, general manager of the National Hockey League's Philadelphia Flyers. They discussed what Hayley could do to take her skills to a higher level. Clarke, recognizing her exceptional talent and drive to improve, invited Hayley to his team's training camp for rookies.

When Hayley arrived in June 1998, reporters swarmed the rink. Players were shocked that a woman was at the camp. Hayley made sure the players and the media knew she wasn't there to take anyone's spot on the team. She was there to measure her skills against NHL rookies.

For two weeks Hayley marveled at how tough, talented and strong these players were. "I had to work hard against the men. I was tough mentally because of all my training,

At the Philadelphia Flyers rookie training camp in 1998, Hayley was the only female.

but I realized these guys go to camp to learn how to work hard on and off the ice." Workouts lasted six to eight hours a day, including four hours on the ice. Hayley loved the challenge and returned in 1999 to test her skills again.

At Hayley's hockey school, the Wickenheiser One on One Tour, she teaches girls on and off the ice.

The following year Hayley began dating Tomas Pacina, a Czech hockey coach assisting the Canadian women's national team. In November 2000, Hayley and Tomas launched a traveling girls' hockey school called the One on One Tour. Hayley wanted to show female players some of the skills and approaches she had learned in her experiences as an elite player. The tour visited 12 Canadian cities and trained over 3000 girls with the help of companies that sponsored the school.

Boyfriend Tomas Pacina and son Noah coming home from the rink after watching Hayley practice.

It was also a special year for Hayley personally. She adopted Tomas's three-month-old son Noah. "It was a huge decision," says Hayley. "I wouldn't have had a child at that point, but Tomas and I were planning to spend our lives together so it was natural that I would become Noah's mom."

Play Ball!

After playing with the NHL rookies, Hayley decided she wanted another challenge. She hoped to become only the second Canadian woman to compete in both the winter and summer Olympics.

Hayley had always played softball as a break from hockey. She loved the fact that the game was played outdoors and was different from hockey. By 15 she'd won the Top Batter and All Canadian Shortstop awards at the National Women's Softball Championship. A year later, in 1995, Hayley made the national junior team.

In 1995 Hayley played shortstop at the Midget National Championship.

As in hockey, finding good competition in Hayley's age category was tough. She commuted from Calgary to Edmonton for two years to play for a senior team. In 1997 she had to return to full-time hockey to train for the Nagano Olympics. When she tried out for the national women's softball team in 1999, she fell short.

"I wasn't ready," Hayley recalls. "It was too soon after Nagano. I didn't have time to train. I told myself if I was going to make the team I'd have to make a bigger commitment."

In August 1999, Hayley moved to Vancouver to train full-time at Simon Fraser University, which has the only women's university softball program in Canada.

Hayley gets a hit for her Edmonton team in 1999.

"I was very focused," says Hayley. "When I was a kid I had dreamed I would play softball in the Olympics."

Hayley's hard work paid off and she made the national softball team. But barely — she was one of the last players picked.

When Hayley arrived in Sydney, Australia, for the 2000 Olympics she felt very little pressure. "Softball doesn't get much media attention. Nobody expected us to do that well," she says. "It was very different from hockey." The team finished eighth in the rankings.

"It was disappointing for the team, but I was proud of the way I played because I came from so far back. I went from being the last player chosen to being a key contributor with one of the highest batting averages."

Practicing with the national team at the Sydney Olympic Games in 2000.

Olympic Fever

Hayley jumped back into hockey full-time in fall 2000. But her playing was cut short by a freak accident. In March 2001, she collided with a teammate at the national championship and suffered a partially torn knee ligament.

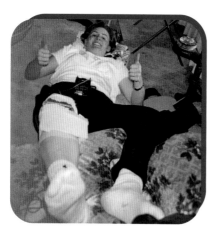

Hayley nursing her swollen knee in spring 2001.

The injury didn't require surgery but Hayley had to sit out the World Championship later that year. Disappointed and frustrated, she threw herself into physiotherapy twice a day. She bounced back and was ready to play again after six weeks.

At the Olympic selection camp for the 2002 games, Hayley was chosen for the national team pool of 30 players who would train together full-time. There was a different feeling about this training camp. All the players and coaches felt they were on a special mission — to avenge their loss in the 1998 Olympics!

Bike sprints at a national team camp in Val Cartier, Quebec, during the summer of 2001.

In June 2001 the team's hard work began in a very different setting: Val Cartier, a military base in Quebec. The routine was intense — three weeks of six to eight hours of activities every day, in the blazing summer heat.

"We knew the days would be long and that not every day would be good," says Hayley. "But we learned to take things in stride."

When the final team was announced on November 20, 2001, it included Hayley as an assistant captain. The players decided their motto was "WAR — We Are Responsible." "We were going to war against our greatest opponent," Hayley says. "To win, we had to be responsible to each other and ourselves."

Training at the Val Cartier military base included an obstacle course meant to test the players' toughness.

Canada struggled in pre-Olympic competition. The team lost seven straight games to the United States, including the final game in January 2002. Hayley was normally quiet in the dressing room after games, but this time she felt she had to speak. She stood up and with a trembling voice

"We put green paint on our faces to have fun and build team spirit," remembers Hayley.

declared, "We have come way too far to lose now. I will not stand on the blue line in Salt Lake and accept a silver medal."

The players on Team Canada arrived at the Salt Lake City Olympics knowing they were the underdogs against the United States. They also knew they wouldn't be tested in their first three games. Kazakhstan fell to Hayley and her teammates 7–0. Then Canada beat Russia by the same score, and Sweden went down 11–0. Hayley notched seven points in the three games.

But in the semi-final game against Finland, Canada was trailing 3–2 going into the third period. "Everyone was calm in the dressing room," Hayley says. "We talked about how this was another step we had to overcome. I also knew I had to be a leader." She tied the game with a breakaway goal (her second goal of the game) and Canada went on to win 7–3.

The Finnish team hit the ice flying in the semi-final game. Hayley rushes the net ready to fire another goal.

That win put Canada in the gold-medal game against the United States. In the first period Canada scored once and received four penalties versus two for the United States. The Americans tied the game in the second period. Then Hayley snagged a perfect rebound from a Danielle Goyette shot. "It was slow motion for me," she remembers. "The puck was perfectly placed."

The gold-medal game against the United States was hard-hitting and filled with a lopsided number of penalties against the Canadians.

Canada now led 2–1, but for almost half the second period the Canadians played short-handed, overcoming five penalties versus one for the American team. To the fans, it looked as if the Canadian team was receiving a lot of unfair penalties.

"The number of penalties seemed unbelievable. We were laughing because it was so ridiculous. It became a source of stress relief," Hayley sighs. Despite the penalties, Jayna Hefford scored just before the second period ended, making the score Canada 3, United States 1.

"We went nuts. It was the greatest team effort all year."

In the third period, Canada's penalties continued but fierce forechecking and goalie Kim St-Pierre's miraculous saves kept the States to just one goal. When the final buzzer sounded the score was 3–2. Canada had won its first Olympic gold medal!

"Every single player gave her absolute 100 percent. We saved it for the right moment."

The Thrill of Gold

After celebrating with her teammates and family in Salt Lake City, Hayley drove home to Calgary with Tomas. Canada was gold-medal crazy. "When we hit the Canadian border you could feel the emotion," remembers Hayley. "People had Canadian flags in their cars. Two guys recognized us and started waving flags and honking horns."

Hayley shows off her first Olympic gold medal after a hard-fought game against the United States.

Hayley's scrapbook is crammed with letters of congratulations from fans, politicians and even celebrities such as The Tragically Hip and country singer Terri Clark. Gold-medal fever was everywhere. Hayley received phone calls and requests for interviews daily.

Men's Olympic team managers Kevin Lowe (left) and Wayne Gretzky congratulate Hayley after the women's gold-medal game.

Players gather on the ice for one last time in Calgary after returning from the Salt Lake City Olympics.

Several months later, Team Canada was honored at a fan rally in Toronto. The Sports Network (TSN) broadcast the presentation of the players' Olympic rings at the Hockey Hall of Fame.

For the first time in the history of the women's game, players received additional money directly from a sponsor. Each was given $20 000 from Molson to help make up for the salaries they had lost during the eight months they were away from work.

For six months after the Olympics, Hayley traveled to schools across Canada. She talked about facing adversity and working as a team. She also made sure she carried one very important object. "I always take my gold medal with me. It's meant to be touched. Some kids put it around their necks."

In March 2002, Hayley's hometown, Shaunavon, planned a special homecoming weekend for her. Events included a hockey game to raise money for the local rink. The competition was between a local team and some of Hayley's Olympic and Oval Xtreme teammates.

At a banquet the next evening, Wally Kozak, one of Hayley's Olympic coaches, talked about her intensity and discipline: "She always does her best, always pushes herself. I think she is exceptionally gifted and very intelligent."

Hayley spoke to the audience about training, competing and the thrill of winning gold. "I never thought I would ever have a chance to win a gold medal. Things like that can really happen to a girl from a small town of just 1800 people."

Hayley's Words

"Many times I had to dig deep and perform. All of that adversity helped me and drove me to want to be the best."

"I was the only girl out there and I had to give my best every day. Anything less wasn't successful. I had something to prove."

"Hockey is my destiny — something I was born to do. I realized it was something I was good at and I liked it."

"People would say, 'Girls don't play hockey. Girls don't skate.' I would say, 'Watch this.'"

"With me, coaches always know what they're going to get: lots of intensity, hard work, making things happen, always a threat. That's my ideal as a player."

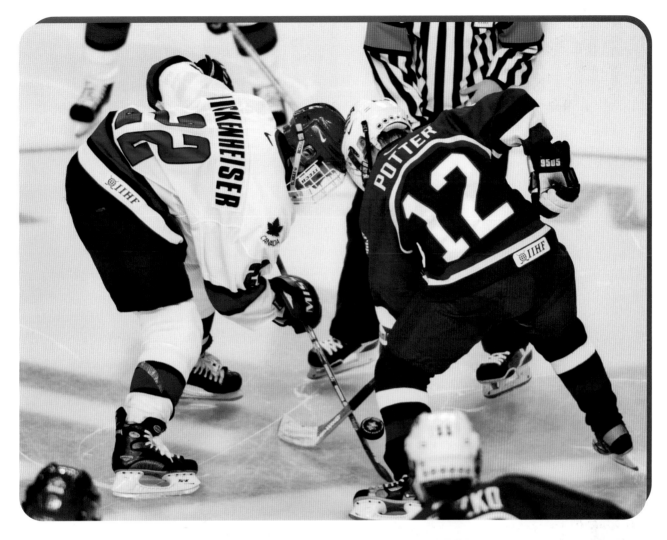

"I struggle against the odds since I'm a female in a male-dominated sport. I believe every girl should have the opportunity to play the game and someday play in a pro league."

"Why do I wear number 22? My best friend Danielle was number 2, so I chose 22. Also Mark Messier wears number 11 and Gretzky was 99 — with 22, I'm in between their numbers."

Doing the Impossible

The Olympics were over and a year had passed. Now what?

"I was at a stale point in my career," remembers Hayley. "I needed to get uncomfortable again. Sometimes you have to get out of your comfort zone before you can really improve."

Hayley thought she'd get the biggest challenge from playing in a men's pro league. North American men's hockey wasn't an option because hitting is a big part of the game. Hayley didn't want to risk injury and knew she wasn't big enough to compete. Instead, she looked to Europe, where the emphasis in men's hockey is on passing and skating — skills Hayley knew she had.

"I never thought a woman could be that good," said Coach Matti Hagman. "Hayley passes better than 80 percent of the team and her slapshot is harder than more than half the players'."

In January 2003 Hayley got her chance. HC Salamat, a men's pro team in Kirkkonummi, Finland, offered her a three-game tryout. Sponsors agreed to pay Hayley's expenses but, unlike her teammates, she received no salary.

When Hayley met the other players they seemed a little uneasy. "They were all quiet and respectful," she smiles. "But I think they thought it was a joke."

It was no joke. More than 80 international reporters attended Hayley's first game. This was hockey history — Hayley was the first North American woman to play forward on a men's pro team. Hayley changed in the referees' room, trying to stay calm despite the pressure. "All day I kept telling myself, 'You can do this. Enjoy the moment.'"

Then Hayley joined her team in the dressing room. Before the players headed onto the ice, one yelled out, "Let's go, Hayley!" and all the players tapped her on her leg. "It meant the world to me," says Hayley. "They wanted me to do well. Plus they were thrilled to be on Canadian television."

The team won 7–3 and Hayley made history. She notched an assist — the first point scored by a female player in a men's pro hockey league.

Hayley checks a Finnish male player while keeping an eye on the play.

Reporters from many countries followed Hayley's history-making activities in Finland.

It was lonely in Finland without family or friends, and Hayley didn't speak the language. But she had some special fans. Ten-year-old Matilda Nilsson, whose parents managed the arena, showed up at every practice and all the hockey games.

Flowers for Hayley from special Finnish fan Matilda Nilsson.

Hayley spoke with Matilda and got to know her family. "They became a support system for me. It was hard being away from my family. I tried to keep myself busy during the days, but the nights were tough. I kept telling myself, 'This is what you have always wanted to do.'"

Both HC Salamat and Hayley soared. Fans flocked to the games, doubling ticket sales and chanting "Heli" when they wanted her on the ice.

Team manager Markku Kulmula talks with Hayley during a practice in Kirkkonummi, Finland.

Hayley gets a push from an opposing player during an exhibition game in fall 2003.

Hayley's ice time averaged around 11 minutes a game. She was killing penalties and sometimes was part of the power play. "I felt like I helped the team," says Hayley. "I loved playing tough games." In just 23 games, Hayley notched 10 assists and 2 goals. The team won their championship series and moved up to the Division 1 League. Hayley headed back to Canada for the summer to rest and be with her family.

In August 2003, Hayley was invited back to Finland to try out again. In seven exhibition games she tallied four points and then accepted a one-year contract. But things were different. The league was better. The promotional advantages of a woman playing with men had worn off.

Hayley was getting very little ice time and her coach's attitude had changed. It seemed that he wasn't interested in having a woman on the team anymore. "I wanted to win the coach over every game and every practice with my hard work, but I knew it wasn't going to happen," Hayley remembers. "Things weren't changing, no matter how well I played."

Looking to score, Hayley is in the center of the action against her Finnish competition.

Coming Home

Hayley had to make a tough decision: put up with a coach who didn't seem to want her or return home, leaving behind her dream of playing men's pro hockey. She decided the little ice time she was getting wasn't worth the separation from her family. On November 23, 2003, Hayley returned to Canada.

"I didn't get enough opportunity to play the role I had my first year. I wasn't happy. I missed my family a lot. I had a chance to play on a different team in the same league, but I decided it was the right decision to come home."

Back in Calgary, Hayley joined the Oval Xtreme, the only senior women's team in the city. The team lost the Esso Women's National Hockey Championship in March 2004, but Hayley tallied 11 points and was named Most Valuable Player in the tournament.

Hayley's approach to the women's game has changed because of her experience in Finland. "I see things a little differently," she says. "I've played the game at a higher level. I've learned to appreciate the game a little more. I'm more patient and better at seeing the bigger picture."

Hayley made Canada's national team again for the 2004 World Championship in Halifax, Nova Scotia. Canada easily swept by its early opponents, Germany and China. But then the team lost 3–1 in a hard-fought game against the

Hayley heads down the ice during a play-off game with her Calgary Oval Xtreme team.

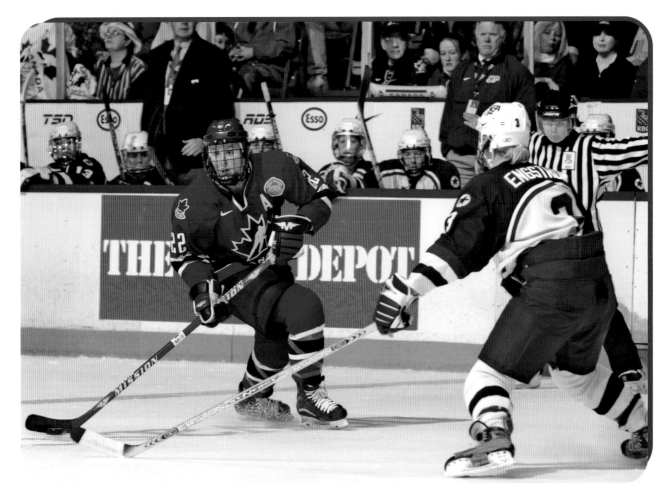

About to pass to a teammate in the final game of the 2004 World Championship.

United States. However, Canada bounced back to beat Sweden 7–1.

That win guaranteed Canada a match-up against the States. In the final game, Hayley slapped a bullet into the net to score the game-winning goal. Canada beat the United States 2–0 to win its eighth World Championship. Hayley notched seven points in the tournament and won the Most Valuable Player award in the gold-medal game.

With Cassie Campbell (center) and Vickie Sunohara, Hayley celebrates their win at the World Championship in Halifax.

What's Ahead?

Most people would agree that Hayley is approaching the peak of her hockey career. So what's next? Will Hayley go back to Finland to play men's hockey?

"I won't consider going back until after the 2006 Olympics," Hayley promises. "I'll always keep the door open if that's what I have to do for myself and my career. I won't do it again, though, without my family being involved."

Hayley definitely plans to keep playing until the 2010 Olympics in Vancouver. "It could be my last Olympics, I don't know. I started my career inspired by the 1988 Olympics. It would be fitting to end my career playing in Canada."

Hayley thinks she has gained a better perspective on the game. "When you play at a very high level, you have to take every opportunity to score because they don't come as often," she says. "I am hungrier around the net. I have a new motivation to keep playing."

Hayley at a skating session with her 2003 team HC Salamat in Finland.

Working on her upper body strength at the Calgary Olympic Oval during summer 2004.

Besides training and competing during the hockey season, Hayley continues to work on her Bachelor of Science degree with the goal of becoming a doctor. "I know it's a lot of hard work but I haven't ruled it out," she admits.

Hayley would also love to play in a women's pro league. "I'm really interested in growing the women's game to a high enough level that the players would be paid. I think I'll have a role in creating a professional league."

What advice does Hayley have for girls who want to play on the national team? "Watch the best players, male or female. Learn all the positions and be a great skater. Be able to read the game and see plays before

At a family farm near Lumsden, Saskatchewan, Hayley lifts tires at her homemade gym.

they happen. I think anyone can achieve anything as long as they love what they do and are motivated enough to do the hard work that others aren't willing to do."

After playing a game for the Oval Xtreme, Hayley signs autographs.

Hayley Wickenheiser's discipline and fierce determination have propelled her to a hero's status in a sport where girls were not, and often still aren't, welcome. She has proven that women can not only play — they can be superstars.